Moon Festival wishes

JILLIAN LIN

Illustrations by SHI MENG

Hi! I am Mei.

Today is a special day for my family.

The moon is big and round tonight.

It is the Chinese Moon Festival.

你好，我是梅。

今天是我家的特别日子。

今晚的月亮大又圆。

今天是中国的中秋节。

We clean and decorate the house.

Pictures of the moon go on the walls.

I make a paper lantern.

Grandma makes yummy mooncakes.

我 们 打 扫 和 布 置 屋 子。
在 墙 上 挂 月 亮 的 图 片。
我 做 纸 灯 笼。
奶 奶 做 美 味 的 月 饼。

I visit the temple with Grandma.

We bow three times and pray.

Grandma says I can make a wish.

What shall I wish for?

我 和 奶 奶 去 了 庙。
我 们 三 鞠 躬 并 祈 祷。
奶 奶 说 我 可 以 许 愿。
我 许 什 么 愿 呢？

It is the night of the Moon Festival.

My family has a huge, delicious dinner.

The food we eat is round like the moon.

And so is my tummy!

今晚是中秋节。
我家吃了一顿丰盛美味的晚餐。
我们吃的食物圆如月亮。
我的肚子也一样！

外面，月亮又大又明亮。
奶奶点了香和蜡烛。
我们向月亮女神祈祷。
我希望她喜欢我们的食物！

Outside, the moon is big and bright.

Grandma lights sticks and candles.

We pray to the goddess of the moon.

I hope she likes our food!

At last, I get what I wish for.

Grandma gives me a mooncake.

I light my new lantern.

Happy Moon Festival, everyone!

最后，我得到了我想要的。
奶奶给了我一个月饼。
我点亮我的新灯笼。
祝大家中秋节快乐！

The End

The Story of the Moon Festival
中秋节的故事

Long ago, the earth had ten suns.

It was very, very hot.

A man in China had a special bow.

He shot down nine suns.

很久以前，地球有十个太阳。

那是非常非常热的。

中国有一男子有一把特别的弓。

他射下了九个太阳。

地球得救了。
人们很高兴。
他们给了这个男子一颗神奇的药丸。
这会让他永生不死。

The Earth was saved.

People were happy.

They gave the man a magic pill.

It would make him live forever.

他的妻子嫦娥吃了那药丸。
她感觉很奇怪。她觉得轻
漂漂的。
不好了！她飞上天了。
嫦娥登月了。

His wife Chang E took the pill.

She felt strange. She felt light.

Oh no! She went up into the sky.

Chang E landed on the moon.

Chang E's husband was very sad.

Each full moon, he prayed for her.

Today, Chinese people do the same.

They call it the Moon Festival.

嫦 娥 的 丈 夫 非 常 难 过。

每 逢 月 圆，他 都 为 她 祈 祷。

今 天，中 国 人 也 这 样 做。

他 们 称 之 为 中 秋 节。

The End

The Moon Festival is also called the Mid-Autumn Festival. To wish someone 'Happy Moon Festival' in Chinese, you would say, *'Jong choh kwai le.'* A mooncake is *'yueh bing'*.

中 秋 快 乐 !
zhōngqiū kuàilè!
Happy Moon/Mid-Autumn Festival!

月 饼
yuèbǐng
mooncake

Around the Moon Festival, you can find lion or dragon dances, markets, and lantern parades in many countries of Asia.

In which countries do you think people celebrate this festival?

在中秋节前后，你可以在亚洲许多国家看到舞狮或舞龙，市和灯笼游行。
你知道哪个国家庆祝这个节日吗？

To celebrate the Moon Festival, people give each other boxes of mooncakes filled with eggs, red beans, lotus seeds, and nuts.

Why do you think mooncakes are round?

为了庆祝中秋节，人们互相赠送盒装月饼。月饼里有咸蛋黄，红豆沙，莲子和果仁。你知道月饼为什么是圆的吗？

Some Chinese stories say that Chang E lives on the moon together with a rabbit.

Can you think of any other festival or celebration that has a rabbit?

有些中国故事说，嫦娥和兔子一起住在月亮上。

你能想想还有哪些其他节日或庆祝活动里有兔子的吗？

Other books by Jillian Lin

Chinese New Year Wishes (3-6 years)
English–中文

Children will follow Hong as he and his family prepare for and celebrate the Chinese New Year festival. They will also enjoy reading the story behind the most important Chinese celebration.

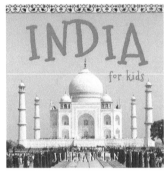

The *Asia For Kids* series (3-6 years) Fun facts and colorful photographs take children on a journey to various countries in Asia and help them discover different cultures.

Also available as e-books on Amazon.
For more information and to get a free e-book, visit
www.jillianlin.com

'A fun way for children to find out about the history of China'

China has a long history, but its many stories are often too complex for children. Jillian Lin has retold these tales so they are easy and fun to read. Children get a glimpse inside the lives of famous Chinese figures including the philosopher Confucius, the first emperor of The Great Wall, and the doctor who invented anaesthetics.

The *Heroes Of China* series (3-6 years) English–中文

The *Once Upon A Time In China...* series (6-12 years)

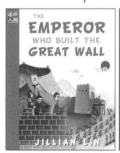

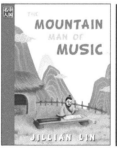

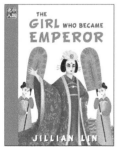

I hope you enjoyed reading this book. If so, I'd be over the moon if you could leave a review!

Moon Festival Wishes

Printed in the USA
CPSIA information can be obtained
at www.ICGtesting.com
LVHW071537270823
756444LV00002B/13